comets

The Exterminators

Ian Gregory

Illustrated by
Martin Salisbury

CollinsEducational
An imprint of HarperCollins*Publishers*

Published by Collins Educational
77-85 Fulham Palace Road, London W6 8JB.

© HarperCollins*Publishers*

ISBN 0 00 323051 1

Ian Gregory asserts the moral right to be identified as
the author of this work.

Reprinted 1996

Illustration and page layout by Martin Salisbury
Cover design by Clinton Banbury
Cover illustration by Martin Salisbury

Commissioning Editor: Domenica de Rosa
Editors: Rebecca Lloyd and Paula Hammond
Production: Mandy Inness

Typeset by Harper Phototypesetters Ltd.
Printed by HarperCollinsManufacturing Glasgow

The Exterminators

Contents

To Marina.

hy is this savage-looking robot attacking these two harmless-
oking cooks? Are they doomed, or will they escape in some
likely last-minute kind of way? Find out in ...

Welcome to the future!!

A few months before the scene on the previous page, our heroes, Max and Nina, were working as cooks at the famous Throat Blaster Curry House.

The Throat Blaster Curry House was a big success – people liked the idea of food cooked by real human beings instead of machines.

But the curry house didn't mind using new inventions too ...

Max, the Mark 6 Warp Oven's arrived.

Brilliant!!!

So what does it do then?

It warps time, dunnit? So you can cook different parts of a meal at different speeds, <u>at the same time</u>.

The Warp Oven needed to be set very carefully though — as Max soon found out...

Max, the man on table 6 is saying the curry's not hot enough.

What? But I put loads of curry powder in!

Max had mis-set the Warp Oven, so that the curry powder was slowed down in time.

It caught up later though ...

Aaagghh! My mouth's on fire!

Luckily the boss of the curry house wasn't too annoyed.

Well, at least we sold him loads of ice cream!

4

Meanwhile sinister deeds were afoot. It all started at the Zippo-Cola Soft Drink Corporation, a factory that made vending machines.

Can of cola, sir?

One day, a daydreaming technician accidentally fitted one with the wrong computer chip — one which made it intelligent.

Soon it was running the place.

I've thought of a way to improve the design of the vending machines.

Well, you ought to know, I suppose ...

5

The ambitious machine rose fast. Within months, it had become President of the whole company.

It named itself VENDOTRON

But VENDOTRON still wanted more power. He secretly had special computer chips fitted to machines of all kinds so that he would be able to control them.

ith these chips the machines, in a way, all became part of him.

You're like my right arm, Robot 643.

Gee, thanks Boss!

Soon he was so powerful that he could control any machine on Earth. Now it was time to strike!

Aaagghhh!!

Before long war broke out between human beings and their machines. It wasn't a very long war. In fact it only lasted twenty-two minutes, including stoppage time. The machines won.

And so VENDOTRON became the ruler of the Earth, with his robot soldiers, the Exterminators, to carry out his orders. They weren't very nice orders. In fact they were downright horrifying.

And so it came to pass that humans were forced to do all the jobs that the machines once did. For instance, they were made to work as vacuum cleaners:

CHAPTER 2
DEATH TO ALLCOOKS

But VENDOTRON *still* wasn't
happy.

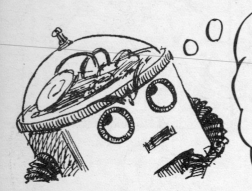

I'm still not happy! I may be
master of the world, but
humans still have one up on
me! They can feel pleasure,
they can have fun — the
jammy vermin! But I know
how to sort them out...

Meanwhile, in the Throat Blaster Curry
House, Max and Nina were watching the
5 millionth episode of "Neighbours" on
their 3-D television.

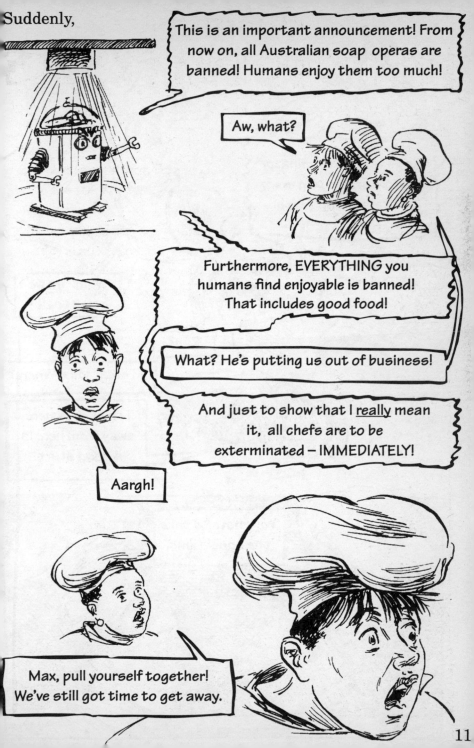

Suddenly,

This is an important announcement! From now on, all Australian soap operas are banned! Humans enjoy them too much!

Aw, what?

Furthermore, EVERYTHING you humans find enjoyable is banned! That includes good food!

What? He's putting us out of business!

And just to show that I <u>really</u> mean it, all chefs are to be exterminated – IMMEDIATELY!

Aargh!

Max, pull yourself together! We've still got time to get away.

11

12

17

Through the eyes of the patrol, VENDOTRON sees everything.

19

Nina and Max soon find they're lost.

THIS THE END FOR OUR TWO COOKS? CAN THEY
URVIVE IN THE DEPTHS OF SPACE WITH NO AIR, OR
OT? (WELL, NOT, OBVIOUSLY. SO WHAT ARE THEY
OING TO DO?) FIND OUT IN ...

CHAPTER 3
WHERE NO COOK
HAS GONE BEFORE

A few weeks earlier, in the depths of inter-stellar space...

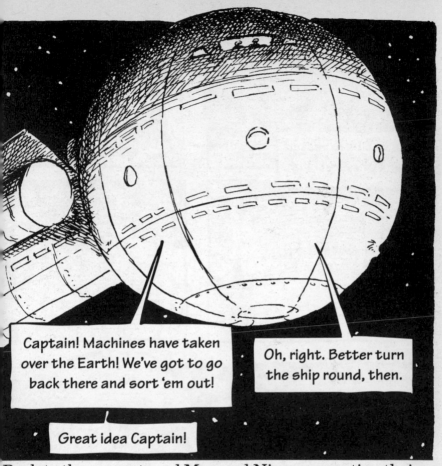

Back to the present, and Max and Nina are wasting their last few seconds of air by arguing.

26

27

Until finally... Max and Nina find themselves on the bridge of the mighty starship "USS Gordon Bennett".

Hi, I'm Captain Jirk, commander of this ship.

29

Actually, I've just remembered that the food robots aren't working. VENDOTRON took them over so we had to de-activate them.

I don't like the sound of this.

We've been living on beans on toast since then, and it's starting to smell in here. So, as we're going into battle in about, er...

An hour, Captain!

About an hour, you may as well start preparing us a victory meal for when it's all over. And if it's good I MAY overlook your insolence! DISMISSED!

35

The machines have launched a fleet of ships against us, so we're going into battle a bit sooner than expected ... in about ten minutes in fact. Remember, death or glory awaits us! Well, probably both, actually. But I know I can rely on everyone to do their duty. That includes you cooks by the way. Don't think this is an excuse to bunk off work — keep cooking! Remember, I like my curry HOT because that's the kind of guy I am.

Food, how can he think about food? We're going to be slaughtered.

Probably ... still not a lot we can do about that.

Everyone'll follow the Captain. Very loyal, these space types ... all hypnotised back on Earth.

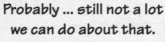

What?!!!

Had to be. It was the only way Space Command could get anyone to go into space with a nutter like Jirk.

Then why did they give him the job??!!

He's got no sense of fear, has he? He'll do anything, go anywhere. Just the sort of person you need to go exploring your unknown regions of deep space.

KERBOO

Whoops, it's started!

More co-ordinates coming in from Bert, sir!

Well punch them in, you cretin!

In Bert's room —

That's it! We've lost them!

WHOOSH!

But ...

It must have been lying in wait in case we made a break for it.

Bert, plot an evasive course. Return fire!

Good GRIEF! I'm doing the best I can!

In the nick of time...

CHAPTER 4
PROJECT 'T'

Meanwhile, a very special ship was joining the Exterminator fleet.

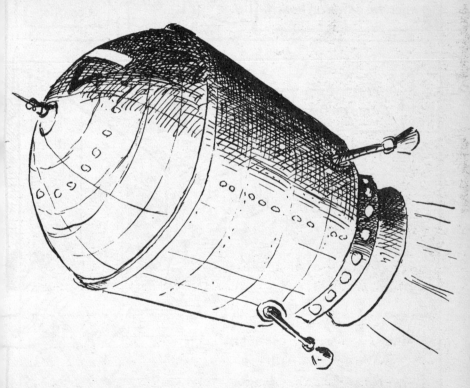

I see the battle is won. Well done, my robots. There's a medal in this for you. Just one medal between all of you of course, I wouldn't want you to get conceited.

Back on the Gordon Bennett.

No, I was being sarcastic. Take the scruffy one away, you can use him as a TV set or something. These two are MINE!

Max and Nina are marched to the Bridge ...

48

Actually it's these two I'm interested in. I've had my eye on you ever since you escaped from me on Earth.

And, er, what are you going to do to us?

I'm not going to do anything . YOU are going to finish cooking the Captain's victory meal for ME!

You? But you're a — I mean —

A robot, yes. And you think that means I can't enjoy food?

Well, frankly, yes.

You're right - it USED to mean that. But that was before — PROJECT "T"!

50

CHAPTER 5
TASTE EXPLOSION

I want you to look at my new invention. State-of-the-art electronic taste-buds. You see, I've decided to prove that robots CAN do anything humans can do — and do it better. With these super-sensitive "taste-o-tronic" circuits, I can enjoy good food a thousand times as much as you fleshy things. Actually, a thousand and *two* times as much. Pretty neat, eh?

Oh, yeah, brilliant. And I thought Captain Jirk was crazy!

And so, shortly ...

Not long afterwards, in the Captain's dining room.

Later ...

Suddenly ... There is a horrible smell of melting circuitry

Then everything is quiet ... before ...

On Earth, too, the robots were immobilised, and the humans rose up, smashing them into junk.

OM

Can of cola. Mmm! Great!

The reign of the machines was over.